TOUCH ME

THE POEMS OF SUZANNE SOMERS

TOUCH ME

THE POEMS OF SUZANNE SOMERS

PHOTOGRAPHS BY
HANK SAROYAN

WORKMAN PUBLISHING
NEW YORK

Original hardcover edition published in 1973 by
Nash Publishing Corporation.

Library of Congress Cataloging in Publication Data

Somers, Suzanne.
Touch me.
I. Title.
PS3569.0652T6   1980   811'.54   80-51893
ISBN 0-89480-141-4

Cover and Book Design: Charles Kreloff
Cover Photograph: Charles W. Bush

Workman Publishing Company, Inc.
1 West 39 Street
New York, New York 10018

Manufactured in the United States of America
First printing October 1980

10 9 8 7 6 5 4 3 2

TO ALAN,
I LOVE YOU

My special thanks to Jim Kavanaugh
for his wonderful inspiration.

FOREWORD

Touch Me was originally published in 1973, long before "Three's Company" was ever conceived and long before I became *Suzanne Somers*. When asked if I would like to see it reprinted, I was very excited because through my public visibility, the poems would get the exposure I'd always wanted them to have. They represent my feelings and emotions as a young woman struggling to grow up in a changing world that, perhaps, I was not ready for.

I love this book. The beauty of poetry is its timelessness, and interesting to me is the fact that although I have grown in many ways, the basic me has changed very little. I am speaking in terms of fears, self-doubt, conviction of self—the importance of motherhood, the importance of the relationship, the importance of feeling comfortable enough with myself to be alone with myself.

It was important for me not to add to this book from my present life—because I wanted nothing to interfere with the purity of these original thoughts. *Touch Me* is my growth and the importance of openness to growth. It is something we all experience; something we can back away from, or something we can embrace with open arms.

I am glad to have the opportunity to share this part of my life with you; and if it can be a source of comfort only in the fact that someone else has experienced similar feelings and emotions, I will feel, indeed, that I have touched you.

Suzanne Somers

INTRODUCTION

Il t is hard for anyone to be ignored. Not to be touched. This is the core of loneliness, life's most acute pain. To wander without contact, without being noticed, without "attention being paid."

There are many ways to touch—lovers touch with tingling intensity, strangers touch with caution, children touch with confidence, competitors touch with suspicion, exploiters touch with clammy hands, the ocean and the forest and the mountains touch with power and gentleness.

We need to be touched, with respect and warmth, with dignity and concern, with passion and understanding. We long to be touched with strength and tenderness, with reverence and beauty, and especially with love.

This is a book about touching—about human hands and arms, eyes and mouths, lives and memories, all the instruments of touch. The cry of the infant reaches out to be touched, life begins with touching, and, hopefully, ends with it. And in between, people pass by—looking, searching, grasping, hoping, falling, rising, and touching —coldly, shyly, angrily, gently, lovingly.

Touch Me is the cry of every voice, of trees and animals, women and men. *Touch Me* is the call of all life, the challenge to death, and to touch and be touched—personally, intimately, honestly—is to live.

TOUCH ME

TOUCH ME

Touch me
In secret places
No one has reached before
In silent places
Where words only interfere
In sad places
Where only whispering makes sense.

Touch me
In the morning
When night still clings
At midday
When confusion crowds upon me
At twilight
As I begin again to know who I am
In the evening
When I see you and I hear you
—Best of all.

Touch me
Like a child
Who will never have enough love
For I am a girl
Who wants to be lost in your arms
A woman
Who has known enough pain to love
A mother
Who sometimes is strong enough to give.

Touch me
  In crowds
    When a single look says everything
  In solitude
    When it's too dark to even look
  In absence
    When I reach for you through time and miles.

Touch me
  In winter
    When darkness comes early
    And the softness of fur surrounds my face
  In summer
    When the sun makes me languid
    And water laps at my feet
  In spring
    When lovers come alive
  In fall
    When the woods call to wanderers
    And dry leaves make softest pillows.

Touch me
  When I ask
  When I'm afraid to ask.
Touch me
  With your lips
  Your hands
  Your words
  Your presence in the room.
Touch me
  Gently
    For I am fragile
  Firmly
    For I am strong

Often
　　For I am alone.

Touch me
　　Not like a cat
　　Or a tree
　　Or even a flower
For I am more than all of these
Yet akin to them: a woman.

Touch me
　　For I was made to be touched.
I can never be touched enough.

TOUCH ME

&

I CAN NEVER BE TOUCHED ENOUGH

REFLECTIONS

I wore my green sweater today—and smiled
    Because there were bits of cockleburs on the sleeve
    And shredded leaves on the shoulders
    A twig or two, and outdoor smells
    And memories of
        Rolling down a hill like children
        Sipping wine and looking out to sea
        Soft kisses on cold grass
        Wind in my hair and sunshine on my face
        Your shirt pulled out and sneakers torn
        Laughing so hard we couldn't breathe.

I wore my green sweater today—and smiled.
    At two weeks ago
        And loving you.

SOMETIMES I WANT TO BE A LITTLE GIRL

Sometimes I want to be a little girl—
    To hear stories of princes
        Kissing sleeping maidens
    And castles towering high on mountains
        Where elegant men
    Waltz with willowy ladies
        To soft violins
    As the stars blink their eyes
        In the glow of the moon.

Sometimes I want to be a little girl—
    To eat popcorn and animal crackers
        And soft, sugary fudge;
    To giggle behind closed doors
        At guessing games and secrets;
    To wear floppy slippers and chew my pigtails
        At ghosts and witches wandering in the night—
    Cuddling beneath howling winds and rain on the roof.

Sometimes I want to be a little girl—
So touch my cheeks lightly
Play with my hair
Stroke me
    Without passion or grasping
    Without expectations
In feather beds and gentleness—
Because I am a little girl.

BEAUTIFUL GIRLS

There are rules
    For beautiful girls to abide by:
You must notice other women
    Or you're a snob
And you must let their men alone
    Because every worthwhile man
        Belongs to someone.
So men stand back
    In deference to their wives
And women stand back
    To watch their husbands.
And only bores step forward
    To tell interminable tales
    And get so close
    And so enthusiastic
That little spitballs fleck your nose.
And even the single guys
    Who look special and exciting
    Stand back and give way to the bores
Figuring that a girl as beautiful as you are
    Certainly wouldn't have any free time.
But you do—lots of it—
    Because there are rules—lots of rules—
For beautiful girls.

EXTRA LOVE

Sometimes I wonder
    If there's enough love to go around.
All the people I know grasp for it
    The ladies whose husbands drift away
    The men whose wives have forgotten to care
    The children standing on their heads to be noticed
And, well, I might as well admit it
    Me—how about me?
Sometimes I wonder if there's enough love to go around
    With all the pain and longing.
But one thing is sure:
    If anyone has any extra love
    Even a heartbeat
    Or a touch or two
I wish they wouldn't waste it.

SOMETIMES I SEE MY SON

Sometimes I see my son
    And remember when I thought I'd failed
    Because so many told me
    A mother who bore a boy
    Should not send away his father.
Sometimes I see my son
    And remember the pain of unloved pregnancy
    And the resentment I sometimes felt
    At raising him alone
    When I could not have the freedom I deserved.
There were days I was as much a child as he
    When I wanted someone to give me
    The love I gave so grudgingly to him.
    Days that we learned together about life
    And had as many questions.
Sometimes I see my son
    And wish his mother had it all together
    To give him strength and courage I only sometimes have
    To listen when my own hurts need hearing
    To hold him even though I am alone.
But sometimes I see my son
    With trust in his eyes no one else could give
    With a smiling, shining face that says there was no failure
    No monstrous mistakes
    Only good things and memories of love and caring.
Sometimes I see my son
    And he touches me in secret corners
    And I know that everything is fine
        And will always be.
    Sometimes I see my son—and I love him.

FOR THE MOMENT

This moment I enjoy
　　Without plans for tomorrow
　　Or distant days too vague and shadowy to know.
This moment I enjoy
　　Without thought of the future
　　Or urgency to understand myself and grow.
My savings are numbered, problems await,
　　Responsibility and fears are never far away.
Time moves swiftly, pain will come again,
　　But God it's great to feel this way today!

TOUCH ME

❧

BEFORE
WE PART

LIES

I have lied to you
    A thousand times
Reshaped the truth
    To keep you close
    And avoid hurting you.
But I always lied with words.

Last night I lied to you
    In silence
    With my hands, my mouth, my caress
The worst lie of all.
    And now I know something is over.
    Because before
I only lied with words.

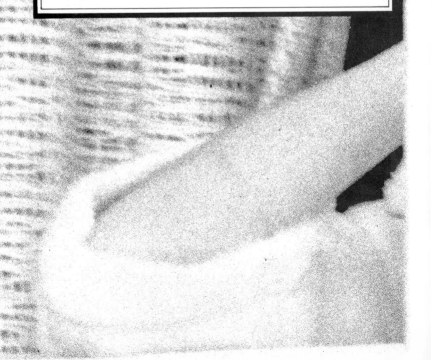

WHEN DID
IT HAPPEN?

When did it happen to us, my darling?
    When did whispers and laughs become silence
    And shared secrets turn to routine words?
We saw it in others, my darling
    Polite arguments erupting in public
    That lonely, haunted look the women take on
    The frequent business trips
    The routine affection, new houses
        and exotic vacations
    That only spoke of emptiness and boredom.
But when did it happen to us, my darling?
    Was it so long ago you brought me flowers
        on Saturday
    When you went to have the car washed?
    You said your body ached for me
    Everytime you saw daisies.
I remember when we made love in redwood groves
        and on beaches
    When there was such lust in your eyes
    As you watched me undress in our bedroom
        and told me to hurry
    As if it were the very first time.
    When TV was only an excuse to lie together
    And a hundred movies never had an ending
    Except in the fullness of our love.

Once while I cooked for you
    I told the brussels sprouts
    I knew you loved them
    Only because you first loved me.
We're so serious now, distant, desperate
    Wounded and wounding, so ready to be apart.
It happens to so many
    Amid children and responsibilities
    Between parties and weed killer and
        hurried breakfasts
Magazines in bed and pills on the nightstand
But when did it happen to us?

THE QUIET LONELINESS OF BEING ALONE

I like the gentle, quiet loneliness of being alone
 Because there's no one special now
 No one irreplaceable like before.
 I have some freedom, some chance to be me.
 There are only voices now, names, responses,
  Kind enough—but not real
 Because I'm not ready.

I like the gentle, quiet loneliness of being alone
 Although I thought of a friend last night
 And almost called
 But I decided not to
 Because my hair needed washing
 And I don't know him well enough
  To look like I really do.

I like the gentle, quiet loneliness of being alone
 Knowing that someday soon
 Something will grow until everything's right,
 Not dramatic glances across crowded rooms—
  I'm nearsighted anyway—
  it'd probably be the houseboy—
  Knowing that I will see in a special way
  And I will want someone to be near.

Meanwhile I like the gentle, quiet loneliness of being alone
 TV in bed
 And dreams
 And smiles
Because I know it will happen
 —someday
 —soon
 —when it's right.

TOUCH ME
IN WHIMSY

ORGANIC GIRL

Organic girl dropped by last night
For nothing in particular
Except to tell me again how beautiful and serene she feels
On uncooked vegetables and wheat germ fortified by bean
    sprouts—
    Mixed with yeast and egg whites on really big days—
She not only meditates regularly, but looks at me
    like I should
And lectures me about meat and ice cream
And other aggressive foods I shouldn't eat.
And she well may be intuitive
Because several times I have thought about cramming her
Unadulterated peace beads down her throat.

It isn't simply that she called my pot roast—
    Simmering in gravy with
        carrots and onions and potatoes—
An accumulation of obscene vibrations
Which could retard my sexuality
Nor did I really mind eating alone—and drinking—
While she munched on celery and crushed almonds—loudly
    I might add—
And fed her puffy little kid mashed avocados and honey
Instead of something pornographic like milk,
Talking incessantly about the beauty of alpha waves,
The thrill of vitamin highs and spiritual excursions,
And the peace that finally hit her after all this searching,

While I was eating pot roast and drinking wine.
Whatever it was, when the aggressive fibers seemed
    to take hold
It suddenly began to dawn on my clogged up cells:
That organic girl and her love-everybody philosophy
Is not nearly as gentle as she is insensitive
    Not nearly as serene as she is bland and boring
    Not nearly as liberated as she is rude and intolerant
And despite her eminent diet and intercourse
    with pure alfalfa—
    Which well may do it for her—
She's damned unhealthy looking!

HOUSE PLANTS

House plants have a way of invading my privacy,
Mimicking my moods, of never leaving me alone,
And I wonder how they changed from potted leaves,
To intimate and privileged members of my home.
Even now, my piggy-back fern, a pale and fragile maiden,
Droops dramatically; as if her life is at the brink,
And I worry that the stereo music displeases her,
Or if I forgot to bring her every-other-daily drink?
Meanwhile kangaroo ivy, an adolescent, now pubescent,
Who only grows higher when I slap him in my wrath,
Smiles knowingly from his lofty perch
And waits to catch me naked from the bath.
Lady sweet potato, who grows a healthy inch each day,
Alone powerless to be desolate or sad.
She's such a joy when I'm in a lilting, happy mood;
But on gloomy days her smile can drive me mad.
And gentle coleus, sensitive artist,
Whose ruddy leaves disguise his fragile life,
Misunderstands my lullabies and soft caress,
And asks me tenderly to be his wife.
Alas! I suppose he will die, while the frilly azaleas
All tin foil and red bows, potted expensively by florists
Will bloom and thrive and long outlive
The more exciting, fragile flowers of the forest.
And why do I hate the African violets?
So hard to grow, so distant and afraid?
Their dry leaves cling like withered fingers to the pot,
And claw at life like whining, sour old maids.

Once I thought that plants were only color in the room
To hide a crack or pick up patterns in the floor,
But now I know they're children, lovers, friends,
They're intimates and enemies and, maybe, something more.
They're victims of my psyche and my moods,
They're friendly, sad, playful, even bitter,
But why when I go out for just one night,
Do they insist I get a baby-sitter?

THE MODEL

The slave traders are out
Walking along the rows of those condemned
    To sell cigarettes and lingerie
    Whirlpool baths and outdoor swimming pools.
The smiling girls, snatched from life
    And frozen into sleek maidens always on display
    Wrapped up, decorated, shaped, and pinched
        through puberty
Cling to their hopes and portfolios
    And confident agents.
(Don't worry, it'll happen, you're gorgeous!)

The slave traders are out
Like some fierce and unrelenting trinity:
The clammy ad exec has gray eyes
    And a dour mouth forever insisting that Cleopatra
    Is not quite right to sell the plots along the Nile.
The squat, dykie lady in the Anne Klein suit
    Takes revenge on the pretty girls
    Who laughed at her pimples and thick thighs in
        junior-high.
    And like some angry magician
    She renders exquisite beauty down
    Into ass and tits and earlobes, and knee shapes
    Calf sizes, skin colors, lip forms, and nose flows.
The fawning assistant, not quite man nor woman
Twitches around like a trapped rabbit
Patronizing, pleasing, whining, appeasing
To put the whole transaction in the right perspective.

The slave traders are out
To sell the American way of life
    With the smiling girl—as soft as Revlon can make her
    Of a hundred takes
    (Show a little tit, babe, bring the man alive)
    And still it's not right
    To sell shampoo and pantyhose.
    (Maybe a single strand of pubic hair, honey, like
        accidental.)

The smiling girl obediently transforms
    Cough drops into sex at the wink of a shutter.
The smiling girl—assembled and reassembled—
    Patiently created each morning to creep back
    Into her skinny portfolio every night.

The slave traders are out
To choose the proper maiden for the job
    And the winner gets an afternoon—or a week of them—
    With clammy and the tight-lipped dyke and
        the fawning court jester.
And if the maiden spends the night on location
    You can bet your properly shaped ass that Mr. Clammy
        will be around.
    If you turn him down he'll probably insist you're
        too plastic to appreciate him anyway—
    Which may damned well be true.
But if you cooperate, that smiling girl selling Winstons
    May look a little like you.
And you'll be paid well to handle rent and the rising cost
    of living
Until the next time the slave traders hire you
    To sell the American way of life.

HANGOVERS

Once
Hangovers troubled me
    And vague memories
        Of loud laughs
        And lewd dances
        And hostile glances
            from jealous wives.

Once
Hangovers troubled me
    And vague memories
        Of insults
        And confrontations
        And things I wanted to say
            but knew I shouldn't.

Now
I enjoy my hangovers
    And vague memories
        Of my vulgarity
            Or whatever,

Because
    I've grown old enough to know
    That everyone has the right
    Once in awhile
To make an ass of himself.

TOUCH ME
IN PASSING

TWO WEEK LOVE

Sometimes when I am sad
    And life is not what it seemed
        And even sex is like a song I've heard
        too often
    I remember my two week love.
    We talked so freely that night we met
        But when I came to you the next day
        It seemed so contrived—the spontaneity was gone—
        My underwear selected carefully
        Nervous blotches on my neck
        A choking voice full of clichés
        And that stupid smile on my face—
        Until you opened the door and I felt the magic
        Despite your suddenly fumbling hands
        The nervous cough
        Your perfectly creased, coordinated casuals—
        And that stupid smile on your face.
    We parried for a time
        Suggesting movies or a ride in the country—
        A study in awkwardness—
        Until someone made a move
        And we were making wild and crazy love
        Before the ice had settled in our drinks.
    It was only two weeks
        But we loved
        God, how we loved
        Until you had to go back home
        With gifts for the children.

And though it's hard to remember your name
    And even your face
    I remember it was really beautiful
    each time.
    When you left my body tingling.
And I remember
    To resurrect
    That love
    Sometimes
When I am sad.

ONLY FRIENDS

We met in the laundromat
  And agreed that
  It's nice to live where there are seasons
  Fresh baked bread is better in winter
  Children need to be left alone
  Presidential candidates have no color this year
  Cocktail parties are a drag
  Camping in the hills is a happening
  Small restaurants are more fun than big ones.
We met in the laundromat
  And laughed at little things
  Like tiny ladies with big cars
  And people who look like their dogs
  And doctors who never smile
  And wives who refer to themselves as "John and I."
It was a special time
  For an hour
  And I winced when you asked for my phone number
  And wished you hadn't
  Because I didn't want it to be
  Anything more
  Than a nice way to spend an hour.

LAST NIGHT IT WAS RIGHT

Last night it was right
  I was lonely, uncertain
  And George was out of town
  I wanted you
  I needed you
  (Or thought I did)
  To feel whole again.
But today
  George is back
  And mother's coming for dinner
  And life moves on
  So I really hope you won't call
  Because
  Last night (for whatever reason)
  It was right.

SOME OTHER TIME

We should have met some other time.
    Right now our heads are clouded
    With only half-forgotten memories
    That make us drift away.
I could be all those things for you.
    Sometimes I want to be
    Even now I miss you when you're gone.
    But not enough.
We should have met some other time.
    You're not one to toy with nor am I.
    You don't play second string so well. Nor do I.
    So we'll probably drift away, knowing
We should have met some other time.

NO!

I don't give you time
>   Because you're a cliché
>   I meet a thousand times a day.
There's no need to talk.
>   I know you're handsome
>   And successful
>   And extremely good in bed.
But really there's nothing to say,
Only a kind of game to play.
>   Only a tedious cliché
>   I meet a thousand times a day.
And I always forget your name.

TOUCH ME

ALWAYS

MAYBE TONIGHT

Maybe tonight I'll tell him that I love him
    When we're alone by the fire and the music is soft
    When he holds me quietly and caresses my hair
    When he touches my breast and his kisses are
        tender and warm.
Or maybe tomorrow I'll tell him
    When we run across hills and rest on rocks
    When the sun warms our bare backs and the wind
        is still
    When we laugh in restaurants and sip red wine
    When we walk through city streets and mumble in
        coffee houses
    When we dream of mountain cabins and the ranch
        we'll build.
Or maybe I'll tell him in the morning
    When we wake from sleep and touch
        without words
    When the smell of toast and coffee is in the kitchen
    When he sings in the shower and lures me
        back to bed
    When we cannot touch enough and listen
        to the rain.
Or maybe I'll never tell him
    Maybe I'll never tell him
    Because time and memories have me wonder:
        If you fall in love with your lover,
            Does it spoil everything?

SIGNALS

We lay there giving signals
    Gently and fearfully
And ended up making love when we only wanted
    A time for tenderness and touching.
I was trying to please you
    And you were trying to please me.
I used to sleep with this guy
    Who always sweetly asked me
When lovemaking had cooled to conversation:
    "Did I please you?"
Clinically, he asked, like putting wallpaper
    On the west wall
    Or adjusting the books on the shelf.
You're not so clinical, but you ask
    God, you ask.
Some night, I wish you would forget me
    Lost in me
    Torn by me
    Soothed by me
    Merged with me
Then, indeed, you would please me.

A CHILD

It's okay to be a child tonight, my love
    Weak and tired in my arms
    Too weary to hold up your head.
    Be the way you feel, my love
    Give in to your tears!
    Let go! The enemy's gone
    And I am here
        To muss your hair
        And stroke your skin
        And hold you close against my breasts.
It's okay to be a child tonight, my love
    No battles to win or worlds to conquer
    Not strong and powerful.
    Let me be whatever you need, my love
    Give in to your pain
    Let go! The enemy's gone.
    And only I am here
        To hold you
        And fondle you
        And love you like a child.
It's okay to be a child tonight, my love
    I already know the man
        You scream him so
        And drive him so
    But don't hide the child from me
    Let him appear—in my arms—without fear
    Because I already know
        And love you.

CLOSE TO YOU

I really felt close to you last weekend
    It was nothing spectacular
    Or easily explainable.
Outsiders wouldn't understand
    But the meals we cooked
    And the love we made
Seemed to grow
And flow like silent songs.

I have known times
    When Acapulco was a humid bore
And Hawaii the monotonous lapping of waves
    Keeping pace with the pointless talk
      Of pointless people;
Times when the glowing ads were calculated lies.

Maybe it's timing—or maybe it's love
    I'm hard pressed to know what or why—
    But last weekend—a very ordinary weekend—
    I really felt close to you.

LITTLE THINGS

There are moments
    When you look at me
    Hold me close
    And I know I love you.
But the moments
    That mean the most
    Are when I look at you
    And you don't know
    I am looking,
    When you ask nothing
    And get everything
    I have to give.
I'll remember the times you looked into my eyes,
But most of all
    I'll remember watching you
        Reading
        Or fooling with the dog
        Or cooking on Sunday morning
        Or brushing your teeth
And knowing
    That I love you.